## Presidents

# CALVIN COOLIDGE

## A MyReportLinks.com Book

Amy Graham

# MyReportLinks.com Books

### an imprint of

 **Enslow Publishers, Inc.** **E**

Box 398, 40 Industrial Road
Berkeley Heights, NJ 07922
USA

MyReportLinks.com Books, an imprint of Enslow Publishers, Inc.

**Library of Congress Cataloging-in-Publication Data**

Graham, Amy.
  Calvin Coolidge : a MyReportLinks.com book / Amy Graham.
    p. cm. — (Presidents)
Includes bibliographical references and index.
Summary: Discusses the personal life and political career of the man who
became the thirtieth president of the United States in 1923 upon the
death of President Harding. Includes Internet links to Web sites, source
documents, and photographs related to Coolidge.
  ISBN 0-7660-5015-7
  1. Coolidge, Calvin, 1872–1933—Juvenile literature. 2.
Presidents—United States—Biography—Juvenile literature. [1. Coolidge,
Calvin, 1872–1933. 2. Presidents.] I. Title. II. Series.
  E792 .G73  2002
  973.91'5'092—dc21

                                                    2001004267

Printed in the United States of America

10 9 8 7 6 5 4 3 2 1

**To Our Readers:** We have done our best to make sure all Internet addresses in this book
were active and appropriate when we went to press. However, the author and the publisher
have no control over and assume no liability for the material available on those Internet sites
or on other Web sites they may link to. Any comments or suggestions can be sent by e-mail
to comments@myreportlinks.com or to the address on the back cover.

**Photo Credits:** © Corel Corporation, pp. 1, 3; Courtesy of Calvin Coolidge
Memorial Foundation, pp. 12, 15, 25, 28; Courtesy of Grolier Encyclopedia
presents The American Presidency, p. 13; Courtesy of MyReportLinks.com
Books, p. 4; Courtesy of The American Presidency: A Glorious
Burden/Smithsonian National Museum of American History, p. 37; Courtesy of
the University of Virginia, p. 43; Courtesy of The White House, p. 40; Courtesy
of Vermont Historical Society, pp. 16, 18, 21, 30, 31; *Dictionary of American
Portraits*, Dover Publications, Inc., © 1967, pp. 1, 27, 34, 38; Library of
Congress, pp. 22, 32, 33, 36, 42.

**Cover Photos:** © Corel Corporation; Painting by Charles S. Hopkins/White
House Historical Association.

Tools

Search

Notes

Discuss

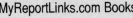
MyReportLinks.com Books

Go!

# Contents

# MyReportLinks.com Books
### Great Books, Great Links, Great for Research!

MyReportLinks.com Books present the information you need to learn about your report subject. In addition, they show you where to go on the Internet for more information. The pre-evaluated Report Links, listed on **www.myreportlinks.com**, save hours of research time and link to dozens—even hundreds—of Web sites, source documents, and photos related to your report topic.

**To Our Readers:**
Each Report Link has been reviewed by our editors, who will work hard to keep only active and appropriate Internet addresses in our books and up to date on our Web site. However, the author and the Publisher have no control over, and assume no liability for, the material available on those Internet sites, or on other Web sites they may link to.

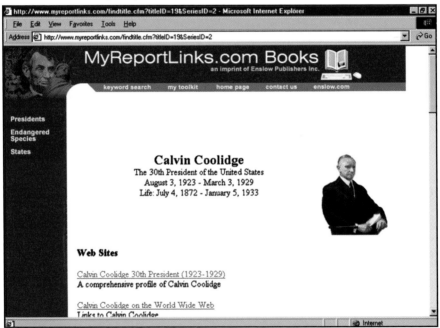

**Access:**
The Publisher will try to keep the Report Links that back up this book up to date on our Web site for three years from the book's first publication date. Please enter **PCO1633** if asked for a password.

## Report Links

The Internet sites described below can be accessed at
**http://www.myreportlinks.com**

▶ **Calvin Coolidge 30th President (1923–1929)**    *EDITOR'S CHOICE
The American Presidents series covers Calvin Coolidge's life before,
during, and after his presidency. You will also find links to his domestic
and foreign affairs.

Link to this Internet site from http://www.myreportlinks.com

▶ **Calvin Coolidge on the World Wide Web**    *EDITOR'S CHOICE
The JFK Library Web site provides numerous links to information
about Calvin Coolidge, including links to biographies, speeches,
quotations, images, sound files, and links to information about
the 1920s.

Link to this Internet site from http://www.myreportlinks.com

▶ **Calvin Coolidge: 30th President of the United States**    *EDITOR'S CHOICE
The official Calvin Coolidge Memorial Foundation Web site was
established to help preserve the memory of Coolidge's life and career.
This Web site offers a wealth of information about Coolidge and his
years of public service.

Link to this Internet site from http://www.myreportlinks.com

▶ **Calvin Coolidge, 30th President of the United States**    *EDITOR'S CHOICE
Presidents of the United States (POTUS) provides a quick reference
profile of Calvin Coolidge where you will find historical documents,
election results, and links to biographies on Coolidge and his
cabinet members.

Link to this Internet site from http://www.myreportlinks.com

▶ **Coolidge, Calvin**    *EDITOR'S CHOICE
DiscoverySchool.com provides details about Calvin Coolidge's early
life, political and public activities, and his life after the presidency.
Learn how Coolidge's Inaugural Address was the first to be heard over
the radio.

Link to this Internet site from http://www.myreportlinks.com

▶ **Calvin Coolidge Became President August 3, 1923**    *EDITOR'S CHOICE
This site explores the Coolidge administration and the Jazz Age. You
will learn interesting facts about Coolidge and the time period.

Link to this Internet site from http://www.myreportlinks.com

The Internet sites described below can be accessed at
**http://www.myreportlinks.com**

▶**The American Presidency: Calvin Coolidge**
Grolier provides a full account of Coolidge's accomplishments as president, as well as his Inaugural Address.

Link to this Internet site from http://www.myreportlinks.com

▶**The American Presidency: Grace Goodhue Coolidge**
This brief profile of Grace Goodhue Coolidge provides basic information about the life of the first lady.

Link to this Internet site from http://www.myreportlinks.com

▶**Calvin Coolidge**
This site contains a brief profile of Calvin Coolidge, and links to biographies, quotes, pictures, and a time line.

Link to this Internet site from http://www.myreportlinks.com

▶**Calvin Coolidge**
Factmonster provides a concise overview of Calvin Coolidge's presidency.

Link to this Internet site from http://www.myreportlinks.com

▶**President Calvin Coolidge**
This site contains interesting facts, quotes, and a biography of Calvin Coolidge. You will also find links to other resources, important events, a list of his cabinet members, and supreme court appointees.

Link to this Internet site from http://www.myreportlinks.com

▶**Calvin Coolidge**
This PBS site provides a brief introduction to Calvin Coolidge's presidency. You will also find links to additional resources, an original document, and a video clip.

Link to this Internet site from http://www.myreportlinks.com

The Internet sites described below can be accessed at
**http://www.myreportlinks.com**

▶**Calvin Coolidge**
This *Encyclopedia Britannica* biography of Calvin Coolidge covers his
education, family life, and political career from governor to president.

Link to this Internet site from http://www.myreportlinks.com

▶**Calvin Coolidge 1872–1933**
This page offers a short profile of Calvin Coolidge's presidency, and
links to objects related to the president.

Link to this Internet site from http://www.myreportlinks.com

▶**Calvin Coolidge (1872–1933)**
This site asks the question "Who was Calvin Coolidge?" Here you will
learn about Coolidge, from his upbringing in Vermont, to his rise to
the Presidency.

Link to this Internet site from http://www.myreportlinks.com

▶**Calvin Coolidge (1923–1929)**
This site offers a profile of Coolidge's life and presidency. For quick
reference there is an outline of basic facts and important dates,
followed by a detailed biography.

Link to this Internet site from http://www.myreportlinks.com

▶**Calvin Coolidge: 30th President, 1923–29, Republican**
This site offers two time lines charting the life and times of Calvin
Coolidge, and the highlights of his presidency.

Link to this Internet site from http://www.myreportlinks.com

▶**Calvin Coolidge: Inaugural Address, Wednesday,
March 4, 1925**
After the death of Warren G. Harding, Vice President Calvin Coolidge
took over the presidency. A year later, he was elected president on his
own. This site contains the full text of Coolidge's Inaugural Address.

Link to this Internet site from http://www.myreportlinks.com

| | | STOP | | | | | |
|---|---|---|---|---|---|---|---|
| Back | Forward | Stop | Review | Home | Explore | Favorites | History |

**Report Links**

 The Internet sites described below can be accessed at
**http://www.myreportlinks.com**

▶**Discovery School's A-to-Z History: Roaring Twenties**
This site provides an overview of the 1920s. Learn about the years of
prosperity experienced by Americans, and Calvin Coolidge's views on
government and business.

Link to this Internet site from http://www.myreportlinks.com

▶**Founder's Library: The Inspiration of the Declaration**
The Founder's Library contains Calvin Coolidge's speech, "The Inspiration of
the Declaration" given on the 150th anniversary of the Declaration of
Independence.

Link to this Internet site from http://www.myreportlinks.com

▶**Grace Anna Goodhue Coolidge 1879–1957**
The official White House Web site contains the biography of Grace
Anna Goodhue Coolidge. Described in this biography are the first
lady's accomplishments, and her life before and during Calvin Coolidge's
presidential term.

Link to this Internet site from http://www.myreportlinks.com

▶**John Calvin Coolidge, 30th President**
This concise profile of Calvin Coolidge provides interesting facts about him
and his presidency.

Link to this Internet site from http://www.myreportlinks.com

▶**"I Do Solemnly Swear..."**
This site contains a painting of Calvin Coolidge taking the oath of office, and
the text of his Inaugural Address. You will also find photographs documenting
the day Coolidge delivered his Inaugural Address.

Link to this Internet site from http://www.myreportlinks.com

▶**President Calvin Coolidge State Historic Site**
At this site you will learn about Plymouth Notch, Vermont, the birthplace and
boyhood home of Calvin Coolidge.

Link to this Internet site from http://www.myreportlinks.com

Any comments? Contact us: **comments@myreportlinks.com**

**Report Links**

## The Internet sites described below can be accessed at http://www.myreportlinks.com

▶ **Presidents Day Calvin Coolidge**

This site provides basic facts about Calvin Coolidge's education, family life, and political career. You will also find links to other resources on Coolidge.

Link to this Internet site from http://www.myreportlinks.com

▶ **The Price of the Presidency**

This magazine article, originally published in *Yankee Magazine* in 1996, discusses Calvin Coolidge's life, death, and presidential term.

Link to this Internet site from http://www.myreportlinks.com

▶ **Season's Greetings from the White House: The Coolidges (1923–1928) Beginning of a Tradition**

Learn about the Christmas tradition that began during the Coolidge administration, and read Coolidge's Christmas message.

Link to this Internet site from http://www.myreportlinks.com

▶ **Virtual Vermont: Calvin Coolidge (1872–1933)**

This site provides a brief profile of Calvin Coolidge where you will learn about his birthplace Plymouth Notch, Vermont.

Link to this Internet site from http://www.myreportlinks.com

▶ **Voices of the Presidential Election of 1920**

In the presidential election of 1920, Calvin Coolidge campaigned as Warren G. Harding's running mate on the Republican ticket.

Link to this Internet site from http://www.myreportlinks.com

▶ **The White House: Calvin Coolidge, Thirtieth President 1923–1929**

The official White House Web site provides a profile of Calvin Coolidge, where you will find interesting facts about his life and career.

Link to this Internet site from http://www.myreportlinks.com

## Highlights

**1872**—*July 4:* Calvin Coolidge is born in Plymouth Notch, Vermont.

**1885**—Calvin's mother, Victoria, dies.

**1890**—Abbie, Calvin's younger sister, dies from what was probably appendicitis.

**1895**—Graduates from Amherst College.

**1898**—*Dec. 7:* Elected to the Northampton, Massachusetts, Common Council.

**1899**—Named Northampton city solicitor.

**1903**—Appointed Northampton Clerk of Courts.

**1905**—Marries Grace Anna Goodhue in Northampton, Massachusetts.

**1906**—*Sept. 7:* Grace gives birth to their first son. He is named John after Calvin's father.

Elected to the Massachusetts House of Representatives.

**1908**—*Apr. 13:* Calvin, Jr., the Coolidge's second son, is born.

**1909–1910**—Serves as mayor of Northampton, Massachusetts.

**1911–1915**—Serves as a Massachusetts state senator.

**1915**—Elected to serve as lieutenant governor of Massachusetts.

**1918**—Elected Massachusetts governor.

**1920**—Nominated the Republican candidate for vice president of the United States. He and Warren G. Harding win the election.

**1923**—*Aug. 3:* Becomes president upon Harding's death. Takes the oath of office at his father's home in Plymouth Notch, Vermont.

**1924**—*July 7:* The Coolidge's second son, Calvin, Jr., dies from an infection.

*Nov.:* Elected president of the United States.

**1929**—*March:* Calvin and Grace Coolidge retire to Northampton, Massachusetts.

**1933**—*Jan. 5:* Dies at the age of sixty-one from a heart attack.

# Oath of Office, August 1923

In the summer of 1923, President Warren G. Harding was touring the American West. He often stopped and gave speeches to admiring crowds along the way. Some people were worried about the president's health. He had looked tired during the whole trip. President Harding had learned some upsetting news. Some of his friends had stolen oil and money from the government. It would not be long before the whole nation found out. He was sick with worry.[1] While in Alaska, he fell ill with a case of food poisoning. Soon he recovered and continued south to San Francisco.

Calvin Coolidge was Harding's vice president. Coolidge was spending the summer with his wife, Grace, and their two boys. While President Harding saw the West, Coolidge visited his father, John, in Vermont. John Coolidge lived on a farm in a small town called Plymouth Notch. The farm had no electricity. The only telephone in town was at the general store.

On August 2, 1923, Calvin and Grace went to bed early. They had a long day ahead of them. The next day they would be traveling to Massachusetts to visit with some friends. A little after midnight, John Coolidge awoke to someone banging on the front door. He opened the door to find a telegraph messenger. The nearest telegraph office was miles away. The messenger had urgent news from San Francisco. President Harding had died unexpectedly of a stroke.

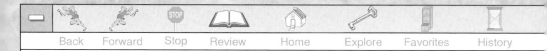

<<Back    **Home**    Next>>

*Son John, Calvin Coolidge, and Colonel John Coolidge, 1916.Plymouth Notch, Vermont.*

photo ©2000 Calvin Coolidge Memorial Foundation

go to CCMF Membership page          Internet

▲ *Coolidge spent many summers at Plymouth Notch. Here he is pictured with his son John, left, and his father John, right, in 1916. It was on this farm that he received the news of President Harding's sudden death and was sworn in as president.*

John Coolidge climbed the stairs to tell his son the news. Calvin heard his father calling to him. He knew something was wrong from the sound of his father's voice. It trembled the way it did when he had bad news.[2] John handed Calvin the official telegram. The vice president was sad to lose his friend and president. He also knew he must now bear the heavy responsibilities of the presidency. Calvin and Grace quickly washed and dressed. Before joining the others downstairs, Calvin Coolidge knelt by his bed to pray. He asked God to bless the American people and to give him the strength to serve them.[3]

The first thing Coolidge did was to write to President Harding's wife, expressing his condolences. He assured her she should stay in the White House as long as she needed. Then he issued a public statement to the reporters who had arrived in Plymouth Notch. He told the American people that he planned to take the oath of office and return to Washington, D.C., right away. He also said he would not make any drastic changes in Washington. Finally, he joined the nation in mourning the much-loved President Harding.

What followed was simple but powerful. At 2:45 A.M. the sky was still quite dark. The small sitting room was lit

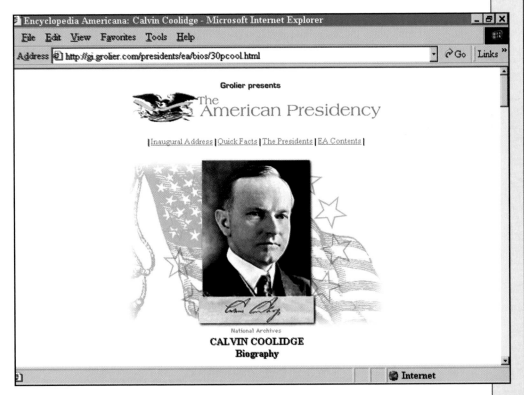

President Coolidge promised to be an honest man and defend the Constitution of the United States.

with kerosene lanterns. Calvin Coolidge found the text of the oath of office in the Constitution. He raised his right hand and repeated after his father, who was a notary public: "I do solemnly swear that I will faithfully execute the office of President of the United States and will, to the best of my ability, preserve, protect, and defend the Constitution of the United States." And then he added, "So help me God."[4]

# Early Years, 1872–1897

**C**alvin Coolidge was born on July 4, 1872, in rural Vermont. He is the only American president to date to be born on Independence Day. Calvin was the eldest child of John Calvin and Victoria Josephine Coolidge. The family lived in a house attached to the post office and general store in the town of Plymouth Notch. Calvin was born in a small first-floor room of the house. In 1875, Calvin's

CCMF Galleries: Selected Photographs - Microsoft Internet Explorer

File   Edit   View   Favorites   Tools   Help

Address http://www.calvin-coolidge.org/pages/galleries/photos/pages/0154.htm   Go   Links

<<Back   **Home**   Next>>

*Plymouth elm tree in front of general store, c.1920's. Plymouth Notch, Vermont.*

photo ©2000 Calvin Coolidge Memorial Foundation

Internet

▲ Here is a picture of the elm tree in front of the general store in Plymouth Notch.

younger sister, Abigail (Abbie), was born there as well. Soon after Abbie's birth, the family moved to a farm across the street.

## ▶ True Vermont Stock

Plymouth Notch was a farming community in the 1870s. Most of the twelve hundred people who lived there worked their own farms to provide food for their families. Farmers raised sheep and other livestock to sell or trade for goods they could not make themselves. Between 1850 and 1880, many Vermonters moved west to find new opportunities, but not the Coolidge family. Calvin and his sister were the fifth generation of the Coolidge family to live in Plymouth Notch. Their great-great-grandfather had been one of the first town selectmen in 1789. Calvin was taught many of his ancestors' beliefs. Most notable of these were that waste is sinful and hard work is valued. The basic principles of living a simple life and saving money for the future guided Calvin throughout his life.

Both Calvin and Abbie attended a one-room stone schoolhouse. By all accounts, Calvin was a typical country boy. No one thought that he would one day play such an important role in United States history. His schoolwork was average. He spent his free time working and playing on the family farm or learning about business at his father's store.

◀ *Here is a photo of young Calvin Coolidge.*

John Coolidge—the sometimes storekeeper, farmer, and schoolteacher—also served in public office. He was an important role model for his son.[1] Calvin was quiet, hardworking, and self-reliant, just like his father. Some even considered Calvin witty.

Calvin's mother died when he was twelve years old. Victoria Coolidge had fallen from a horse-drawn buggy years earlier, was seriously injured, and never fully recovered. Calvin later wrote: "The greatest grief that can come to a boy came to me. Life was never to seem the same again."[2] His family worried about him during the next year, but he continued with work at school and on the farm. At thirteen, Calvin passed his final exams. He had learned all that he could at the small Plymouth Notch schoolhouse. His father decided to send him on to the Black River Academy, twelve miles away in Ludlow, Massachusetts.

## Interest in Politics

Calvin followed the college preparatory path. His courses included Latin, Greek, world and United States history, and mathematics. In his civil government class, Calvin developed a lifelong interest in the Constitution of the United States. He was fascinated with the ancient Greek and Roman civilizations, and he began to develop an understanding of the history of world politics. A physically active young man, on the weekends he would sometimes walk all the way home from school.

The presidential election of 1888 was a much-discussed event at the Black River Academy. Most of rural Vermont supported the Republican candidate, Benjamin Harrison, against President Grover Cleveland, the Democratic

candidate. The election and the celebration when Harrison won helped to shape Calvin's interest in politics.

In March of Calvin's senior year, his sister, Abbie, fell sick with what was probably appendicitis. Calvin went home to be by her side. Little was known about appendicitis in 1890, and Abbie's illness was not properly treated. In a few days she died. Now just Calvin and his father remained.

### ▶ Early Speech Writing

A few months later Calvin graduated from the Academy in a class of nine students. At graduation he gave a speech entitled "Oratory in History." He spoke about the ways people's words had influenced history. After graduation Calvin traveled south to Amherst, Massachusetts, to take an entrance exam for Amherst College. During his trip, he caught a bad cold, probably influenza, and was unable to finish his test. He took the train back home and worked on the farm for several months. The principal at Black River Academy suggested Calvin spend the

◀ *In this letter written a few weeks after her death, Calvin expresses how he misses his sister Abbie.*

spring semester studying at St. Johnsbury Academy, in northern Vermont. At the end of the semester, Calvin was accepted to Amherst College. In the fall of 1891, Calvin Coolidge said good-bye to his father and his new stepmother, Carrie Brown. The two had been married a week earlier.

Coolidge kept to himself in his first two years at Amherst. His junior year was different. He began to attract attention. Professors Anson Daniel Morse and Charles E. Garman may have been the reason for this change. They sparked his interest in government, politics, oratory, and debate. In his senior year, Coolidge submitted an essay to a contest held by the National Society Sons of the American Revolution. The title of the essay was "The Principles Fought for in the American Revolution." He won a gold medal for his first-place entry.

## Coolidge Studies Law

Coolidge decided to study law after graduating with honors from Amherst in 1895. He studied in the law offices of Hammond and Field in Northampton, Massachusetts, not far from Amherst. It was common practice then for lawyers to get their legal training in this way, rather than by attending a law school. Coolidge focused on his work. He wanted to prove to his father that he was worthy of the sacrifices made to send him to college. He passed the bar in 1897, a year earlier than expected. Calvin Coolidge then went on to open up his own law practice in Northampton.

## Chapter 3

# Massachusetts Politics, 1898–1920

Calvin Coolidge thought he would spend his life as a good country lawyer. He became active in local politics because he felt it would make him a better lawyer.[1] Also, his father's example of public service and the encouragement of Hammond and Field had done much to spur his participation in politics. For Coolidge, it was easy to decide which political party to support. He had grown up in a Republican household and town. Coolidge was first elected to serve a one-year term on the Northampton Common Council in 1898. The next year, he was named city solicitor. As solicitor, he provided legal advice to the Common Council until 1902.

## ▶ Man of Few Words

In 1903, the Northampton Clerk of Courts died. Coolidge was asked to take his place until the next election. The position paid well but when election time came, Coolidge decided not to run. His law business began to do well, and he was able to save some money. Then, in 1904 he was chosen as the chairman of the Republican City Committee. Coolidge earned a reputation as a polite listener. While he often kept his thoughts to himself, when he spoke, he said something noteworthy.[2]

## ▶ Quiet Calvin, Outgoing Grace

In 1905, Coolidge met a teacher named Grace Anna Goodhue. Like Coolidge, she was from Vermont. The first time Grace saw him she was walking along the street. Through a window she saw Coolidge shaving. He was wearing only a union suit—a one-piece undergarment—and a hat. The sight of the tall, thin man in his underwear, but still wearing a hat, struck her as being funny. Coolidge heard her laughing as she walked by. They met soon afterwards. Grace was very outgoing and talkative compared to the shy, quiet lawyer.

Later that year they were married. The couple honeymooned in Montreal, Canada. A trip to Havana, Cuba, in 1928 was the only other occasion when Coolidge traveled outside the United States. Coolidge's sense of

▲ *Coolidge used every opportunity to campaign for his seat in the state House of Representatives. This photograph shows him greeting a crowd of young children at the train station.*

▲ *Like his wife Grace, Coolidge supported the rights of women. Here is a parade of suffragists, who lobbied for women's suffrage—the right to vote.*

commitment caused the newlyweds to cut their honeymoon short. He was running for a seat on the school board in Northampton, and he wanted to get back to campaign. Coolidge lost the race. It was to be his only loss in all the times he ran for office.

The following incident offers a lighthearted moment between Grace and Calvin Coolidge. "One day Coolidge arrived home from his office with a bag containing 52 pairs of socks, all with holes. His bride asked if he had married her to darn [mend] his socks. To this the ever blunt Coolidge replied: 'No, but I find it mighty handy.'"[3]

## ▶ State Representative

Calvin and Grace Coolidge moved into a house on Massasoit Street in Northampton. This would be their home for many years. On September 7, 1906, Grace gave birth to a son. They named him John, after his grandfather. Coolidge ran for the state House of Representatives that fall. He went door to door around the district, telling people, "I want your vote. I need it. I shall appreciate it."[4] People liked his straightforward ways. He won the election and left for Boston in January 1907 to serve his term.

During his weeks in Boston, Coolidge rented a room for a dollar a day at the Adams House. On the weekends, he would take the train home to visit his wife and son. Coolidge served two years as a state representative. During these years, he supported many progressive ideas: including, a women's right to vote and a six-day workweek.

## Mayor of Northampton

When his term finished in June 1908, Coolidge returned to Northampton. In 1909, Northampton elected him mayor. During his two years as mayor, Coolidge applied his frugal ways and increased wages for teachers while decreasing taxes. He had the streets and sidewalks paved and lowered the city's debt. It pleased him to be able to spend more time with his family. A second son, Calvin, Jr., had been born on April 3, 1908.

## State Senator

In 1911, Republicans encouraged Coolidge to run for the state senate. He won and went back to Boston. The senate had fewer members than the state house of representatives, and Coolidge was able to take on more responsibilities. Almost every bill he supported was passed. People saw he was honest and productive. He was re-elected for three more terms, and in his third year, he became president of the Senate. The governor and

lieutenant governor were Democrats, making Coolidge the highest-ranking Republican in the state.

## Governor of Massachusetts

During his years in the state senate, Coolidge made a lifelong friend named Frank Stearns. Stearns, a wealthy Boston merchant, was also a graduate of Amherst College. Stearns encouraged Coolidge to run for lieutenant governor. Coolidge ran and was elected to serve from 1916 through 1918. As lieutenant governor, he sat on the governor's council and gave many speeches around the state. In 1918, Coolidge was elected governor of Massachusetts.

## Boston Police Strike

Coolidge's most well-known action as governor was his handling of the Boston police strike. The police threatened to walk off the job if their salaries were not raised. The commissioner told the officers they must not strike. On September 9, 1919, many of the police did not arrive for work. With no one to enforce the law, looting and violence broke out. The National Guard restored order. All the men who had been on strike lost their jobs.

Samuel Gompers, president of the American Federation of Labor, asked Coolidge to let the officers return to work, or give them back their jobs. Coolidge believed the situation called for strong action. Yet, ever a shrewd politician, he knew the consequences of public disapproval. Emotions were high, and everyone had an opinion. Coolidge answered Gompers with a telegram that read, "There is no right to strike against the public safety by anybody, anywhere, any time!"[5] He issued his reply confident the American public agreed with him. They did! Calvin Coolidge became a national hero.

Tools    Search    Notes    Discuss                                    Go!

## The 1920 Republican Convention

In 1920, the Republican Party met to nominate candidates for the upcoming presidential election. For president, they chose Warren G. Harding, a popular senator from Ohio. Deciding on a running mate for Harding was easy. People remembered the Boston police strike. They chose Coolidge as the Republican candidate for vice president. At election time, America was ready for a change now that World War I was over. Harding and Coolidge won by a landslide. Soon Coolidge and his family were packing for Washington!

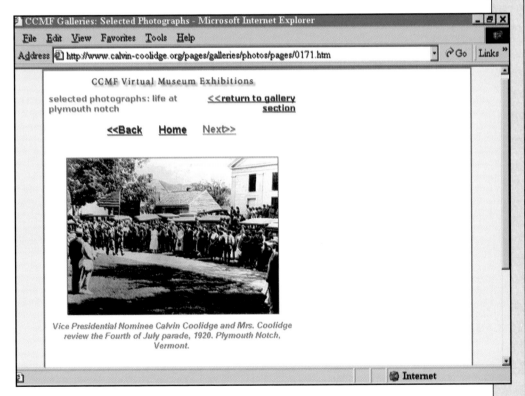

CCMF Galleries: Selected Photographs - Microsoft Internet Explorer

File    Edit    View    Favorites    Tools    Help

Address  http://www.calvin-coolidge.org/pages/galleries/photos/pages/0171.htm    Go    Links

CCMF Virtual Museum Exhibitions

selected photographs: life at          <<return to gallery
plymouth notch                                        section

<<Back      Home      Next>>

*Vice Presidential Nominee Calvin Coolidge and Mrs. Coolidge review the Fourth of July parade, 1920. Plymouth Notch, Vermont.*

Internet

▲ *Coolidge and his wife Grace continued to visit Plymouth Notch even during his administration. In 1920, Coolidge, then the vice presidential nominee, and his wife Grace participated in the small town's Fourth of July parade.*

**Chapter 4 ▶**

# Washington, 1920–1924

While President Harding was moving into the White House, the Coolidge family moved into an apartment in the Willard Hotel. John and Calvin, Jr., were sent to school at Mercersburg Academy in Pennsylvania. Coolidge put all his energy into learning about Washington politics. He had much to discover about how things worked in the capital.

## ▶ Nontraditional Vice President

The vice president is also the president of the U.S. Senate. Coolidge learned a lot from working with the senators. Public speaking is a typical, or routine, duty of the vice president. Coolidge took pride in writing his own speeches, even though writing them did not always come easily.[1] Traditionally, the vice president did not have many responsibilities. President Harding thought the vice president should play a more active role than in the past. He invited Coolidge to attend Cabinet meetings. At these meetings, Coolidge learned about how the president runs the country.

President Harding was often too busy to attend social functions. Coolidge and his wife went to many dinners and events in the president's place. Both Grace and Calvin Coolidge enjoyed these opportunities to meet their new community. Luckily, Grace's friendliness offset Coolidge's quiet ways. Coolidge had earned the nickname "Silent Cal." If he did not have anything important to say, he kept quiet. Many people thought his silence was rude at first. Opponents even suggested limited intelligence. However, Americans grew to love stories about Silent Cal's quiet ways and dry Yankee wit. He once commented, "I have never been hurt by what I have not said."[2] Another time he explained that responding "yes" or "no" to other peoples' statements was simply a way to discourage the speaker from continuing.

## ▶ The Teapot Dome Scandal

President Harding gave some friends from Ohio important government jobs. These friends were known as "the Ohio Gang." They enjoyed gambling, smoking cigars, and drinking alcohol—even though the eighteenth amendment to the Constitution had made drinking illegal. The friendly and easygoing president took pleasure in their company.

In the summer of 1923, President Harding died unexpectedly of a stroke. He had been touring the western United States, giving speeches along the way. Coolidge heard the news at his boyhood home in Plymouth Notch. He took the oath of office in the early morning hours on the third of August. All of a sudden, he had become the thirtieth president of the United States of America. Coolidge felt well prepared for the job by his

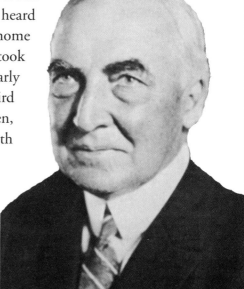

*President Warren G. Harding.* ▶

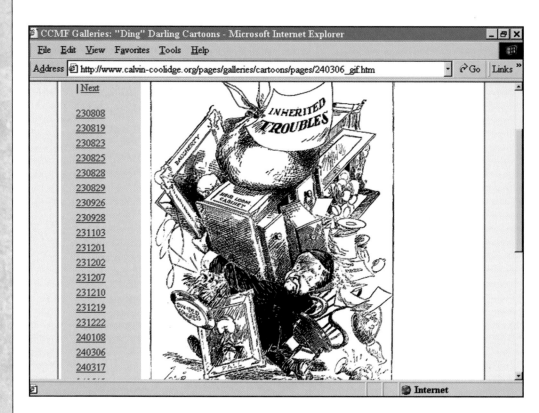

CCMF Galleries: "Ding" Darling Cartoons - Microsoft Internet Explorer

File  Edit  View  Favorites  Tools  Help

Address  http://www.calvin-coolidge.org/pages/galleries/cartoons/pages/240306_gif.htm  | Go | Links

| Next

230808
230819
230823
230825
230828
230829
230926
230928
231103
231201
231202
231207
231210
231219
231222
240108
240306
240317

Internet

▲ After Harding's death, Coolidge had to deal with many scandals from the former president's administration. The most famous was known as the "Teapot Dome Affair."

experience as vice president.[3] He returned to Washington right away to help with the funeral plans. President Harding had been very popular, and the entire nation was in mourning. Coolidge reassured the American people that he would carry on Harding's plans.

Once Harding died, the Ohio Gang no longer had any power in Washington. Congress investigated rumors that Harding's cronies had been stealing from the government. The scandal became known as the "Teapot Dome Affair." One of the worst offenders was Harding's secretary of the interior, Albert B. Fall. Fall had illegally leased government oil reserves in Teapot Dome, Wyoming, to a private oil company. In return, Secretary Fall accepted bribes of cash.

Another person under investigation was Colonel Charles Forbes, head of the Veterans Bureau. Before Harding died, he had heard that Forbes was stealing money, but he had no proof. Congress investigated and found Forbes guilty. Attorney General Harry Daugherty was another one of Harding's Ohio buddies. Coolidge asked Daugherty to resign. Daugherty was later proven guilty of taking part in the scandals.

Coolidge was very popular with most Americans during this time. He had not taken part in these illegal activities. Everyone had heard how he took the oath of office by kerosene light at his father's home. They felt his simple background separated him from the scandals of the Harding era.[4] Shaped by a hard life on a farm, Coolidge had a philosophy of a simple life well lived. He valued hard work, honesty, and self-reliance in overcoming adversity. These beliefs influenced his whole life and shaped his presidency.

## ▶ Issues Facing the New President

In December 1923, Coolidge made his first address to Congress. People were anxious to hear what he had to say. In his speech, he outlined his plan for the upcoming year. Coolidge said it was important to limit government spending. He spoke against the Soldiers' Bonus Bill, which would give soldiers additional money. Coolidge recognized that farmers were struggling, but he did not think the government should get involved. He felt America should not be involved in the international League of Nations. America needed to look after its own issues before helping

other countries. Most importantly, he stressed the need for tax cuts.

This was the first presidential speech to be broadcast by radio. People liked what Coolidge had to say. As he had promised, he had not made any major changes from Harding's plans. The next day, Coolidge's friend Frank Stearns made an announcement. Coolidge would consider running for president.

### ▶ The 1924 Republican Convention

At the Republican national convention in June 1924, Coolidge was chosen to be his party's candidate for president. His running mate was a wealthy Chicago banker named Charles Dawes. The campaign slogan was "Keep Cool with Coolidge." The Democrats had a hard time deciding who would be their candidate. They settled on John W. Davis of New York. There were members

◀ *This is a copy of a letter written by Calvin Coolidge to his father describing his son's illness.*

of both political parties who were unhappy with the candidates. They joined to form a third party called the Progressive Party. The progressive candidate for president was Senator Robert M. La Follette.

During the campaign, Dawes went on a speaking tour. Coolidge, however, did not play an active part. Coolidge had been preoccupied with some personal problems. In July 1924, his sixteen-year-old son, Calvin, Jr., died of an infection. He had been injured while playing on the White House lawn. Heartbroken, the Coolidge family spent the months before the election mourning the death of their youngest child.

△ Several months before the Presidential Election of 1924, Coolidge's oldest son Calvin Jr., died of an infection as a result of a foot injury. Here is a photograph of Calvin and Grace attending their son's funeral in Vermont.

## Chapter 5

# Elected President, 1925–1929

During the 1920s, America grew prosperous. Electricity, telephones, and indoor plumbing came into many homes. New inventions, such as radios, cars, and washing machines changed the way people lived. Factories opened to make these new products, creating jobs. Music and literature reflected the times. Great writers captured the spirit of confidence, and music expressed peoples' enthusiasm. Charles A. Lindbergh, Babe Ruth, Louis Armstrong, and George Gershwin became household names. Children grew up in a time that was very different from their parents' childhood. It was a time of exciting change. The decade became known as the Jazz Age or the Roaring Twenties.

## ▶ A Changing Nation

The president was set apart from this new era. Coolidge stood for saving money while many Americans freely spent money. He led a simple life in which the basics were important. Yet,

*Despite the new changes in society that marked the period of his administration, Coolidge did not adapt to the technology of his day. He even refused to have a telephone in his office.*

▲ *Coolidge supported road construction even though he did not know how to drive a car. During the 1920s, mass production of automobiles was new to the rapidly changing American society.*

American lifestyles were changing rapidly to include new conveniences. Coolidge did not know how to drive a car. Although there were phones in the White House, he did not have a telephone in his office. He felt the president should not talk on the telephone because it was not dignified.[1] Coolidge was the last president to never have flown in an airplane.

Coolidge helped to create the new economy. He kept his promise to lower taxes. By 1927, 98 percent of all Americans no longer paid income tax. While Coolidge did not drive a car, he supported the construction of roads. Highways were built to connect cities and towns. There were many new jobs, and few people were unemployed.

Wages were high. President Coolidge announced, "The chief business of the American people is business."[2] Big American businesses were able to double their profits during these years.

## McNary-Haugen Bill

Not everyone shared the wealth of the times. Small-scale farmers had a difficult time making ends meet. America was growing more than it could sell. Crop prices continued to drop. Some farmers gave up and moved to the cities to work in factories. Other farmers worked together to bring a bill to Congress. The McNary-Haugen Bill was named after two legislators who supported it. The bill called for the government to help solve the farmers' problems. Coolidge's philosophy of self-reliance was at odds with such increased government responsibilities. He vetoed this farm-relief bill in 1927 and another in 1928.

## Kellogg-Briand Pact

Coolidge did not focus on international affairs. Like most Americans at the time, he concentrated on the United States. Still, several important international events occurred during Coolidge's presidency. In 1928, fifteen nations met in Paris and agreed to outlaw war. They signed the Kellogg-Briand Pact and vowed to settle disputes with words, not battles. Many other countries signed the pact later. Coolidge supported the Kellogg-Briand Pact. In fact his Secretary of State Frank Kellogg, was one of the architects of the pact. People rejoiced because they thought that war was gone for good.

*Frank Billings Kellogg, Secretary of State.*

## International Relations

The United States and Mexico were not getting along. Coolidge asked a friend from college, Dwight Morrow, to go to Mexico as the new ambassador. The people of Mexico liked Morrow because he respected their ways. Thanks to Morrow's hard work, relations between the two countries improved. Coolidge had made a wise choice in Morrow.

European nations owed the United States government money as a result of World War I. Coolidge felt strongly that the debt should be repaid. To raise the money, countries sold their goods to the wealthy Americans. The U.S. government required other countries to pay tax on products brought into the United States. These taxes were called tariffs. American tariffs were high. They made it more difficult for European nations to raise enough money to pay their war debts. To ease this burden, the Coolidge administration substantially lowered the interest rates on the debt.

## New Immigration Laws

From its beginnings, the United States had welcomed people from other countries who wanted to make a new start. In the 1920s, Americans changed their tune. Congress passed several immigration acts. These laws sharply limited the number of people who could move to the United States. Americans were scared that people with different beliefs threatened democracy. President Coolidge did not share this fear. He felt America should encourage variety. Whether someone was a new immigrant or a family that had arrived with the pilgrims, Coolidge said, "We are all now in the same boat."[3] Despite his beliefs, Coolidge allowed the immigration laws to pass.

▲ Coolidge welcomed people from different nations to immigrate to the United States. He encouraged the American people to appreciate the cultures of various ethnic groups. Here is a photograph of immigrants on a ship approaching Ellis Island.

## ▶ The Social Years

The Coolidge White House years were full of interesting contrasts. The Coolidge family was very social during these years. They invited more guests to the White House than any president had before. Their friend Frank Stearns stayed with them so often that he had his own suite. On the weekends, Coolidge enjoyed trips on the presidential yacht, the USS *Mayflower*. He would invite friends to join him on a cruise down the Potomac River.

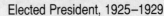

The economy was good, and it just kept looking better. Some Americans began to invest their money in the stock market. These investments paid off as stock prices soared. People began to borrow money in order to invest as much as they could in stocks. Coolidge did not see anything wrong in the rising stock prices. He thought the high stock prices reflected healthy business growth.[4]

## Coolidge Chooses Not to Run

On the fourth anniversary of his presidency, Coolidge held a press conference. He handed a small slip of paper to

First Lady Grace Coolidge was known for her grace and style. Here is a photo of her 1920s flapper dress, which she wore during her husband's administration.

each of the reporters. It read, "I do not choose to run for president in nineteen twenty-eight."[5] The announcement came as a surprise. Even his wife, Grace, had not known of his decision. Coolidge's supporters tried to convince him to run again, but his mind was made up. He would step down and let a new leader come forward. The historian Samuel Eliot Morison asserts that Coolidge secretly hoped his party would draft him to run anyway.

The Republican Party chose Coolidge's secretary of commerce, Herbert Hoover, to run for president. Hoover won the race against Al Smith, a Democrat from New York. On a rainy March day in 1929, Coolidge participated in the inauguration of the new president. Later that afternoon, he and Grace boarded a train home to Northampton, leaving the White House behind.

◀ *President Herbert Hoover.*

# Retirement, 1929–1933

When Calvin and Grace Coolidge arrived at the Northampton train depot, a crowd of people welcomed them home. Tourists flocked by Massasoit Street to see Coolidge in his rocking chair on the front porch. Some people even peered in the windows. The couple quickly realized they needed more privacy. They bought a new home called the Beeches. The grounds sloped down to the Connecticut River. A fence with a gate kept uninvited guests away.

After leaving Washington, Coolidge was offered many different jobs. He was careful to only choose positions that he considered dignified enough for a former president. His first task was to write his autobiography, which was published in 1929. He also wrote magazine and newspaper articles. One year Coolidge wrote a daily newspaper column. He never missed a deadline. Papers from all across the country printed "Calvin Coolidge Says" between 1930 and 1931.

Besides writing, Coolidge agreed to serve on the board of the New York Life Insurance Company. Once a month, he would take the train to New York City to meet with the board of directors. He served as a trustee of Amherst College and president of the American Antiquarian Society, which preserves early American documents and books. He even donated some of his family's belongings to the group.

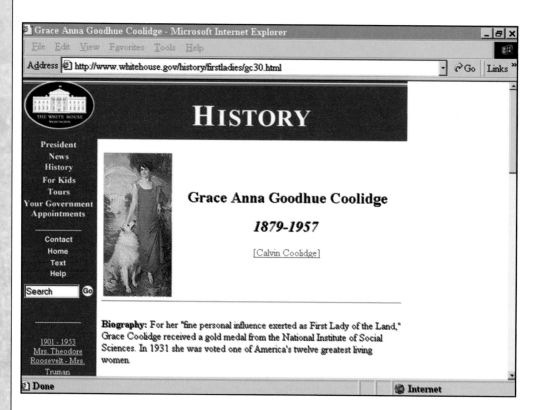

Grace Anna Goodhue Coolidge - Microsoft Internet Explorer

File  Edit  View  Favorites  Tools  Help

Address http://www.whitehouse.gov/history/firstladies/gc30.html   Go   Links

# HISTORY

President
News
History
For Kids
Tours
Your Government
Appointments

Contact
Home
Text
Help

Search  Go

1901 - 1953
Mrs. Theodore
Roosevelt - Mrs.
Truman

**Grace Anna Goodhue Coolidge**

*1879-1957*

[Calvin Coolidge]

**Biography:** For her "fine personal influence exerted as First Lady of the Land," Grace Coolidge received a gold medal from the National Institute of Social Sciences. In 1931 she was voted one of America's twelve greatest living women.

Done    Internet

▲ *Grace Coolidge continued to impress the public even after her husband's administration ended. In 1931, she was voted one of America's twelve greatest living women.*

## ▶ Popular, Despite the Great Depression

Not long after Coolidge left office in 1929, the stock market crashed. America was thrown into a time of poverty called the Great Depression. Later some historians blamed Coolidge for not foreseeing the stock market crash. Others accused him of leaving Washington when he realized the crash was coming. Still, Coolidge remained popular with the American public during the Depression. There had even been some talk of asking him to run for president again in 1932. Coolidge realized his time was over. He said, "I no longer fit in with these times. . . . We are in a new era to which I do not belong."[1]

In the summers, Calvin and Grace Coolidge vacationed at the family farm in Plymouth Notch. Coolidge had a two-story addition built with electricity and a phone. Old John Coolidge had passed away while his son was president. Coolidge thought his father had tired himself out visiting with tourists.[2] During his presidency, thousands of people traveled to Vermont to see where Coolidge had spent his boyhood.

## ▶ Calvin's Simple Ways Remembered

Coolidge would often visit his old law office, now run by a partner. There he would put his feet up on a drawer and read through his letters. People wrote to ask him to attend an event or make a speech. On January 5, 1933, Coolidge returned home from the office earlier than usual. Later that morning, he died unexpectedly of a heart attack. He was sixty-one years old. A funeral ceremony was held in the Northampton Congregational Church. Coolidge was buried in the family plot in Plymouth Notch, alongside his parents, sister, and son.

The death of President Coolidge marked the end of an era.[3] He had been president during a time of great prosperity for America. Now in the midst of the Great Depression, Americans longed for the glamour and excitement of the Roaring Twenties. Coolidge was remembered for his simple ways during a time of wealth and excess. For many people, he represented a way of living that was left behind during the changes of the Jazz Age.

Today the Plymouth Notch homestead is a museum, commemorating the life of the thirtieth president of the United States. After Coolidge died, Grace gave the

This is a familiar scene from the period known as the Great Depression. This famous photograph by Dorothea Lange illustrates how many families lost their jobs and homes and were forced to live in terrible poverty.

property to the state of Vermont. The state purchased other buildings in the town of Plymouth Notch as well. Coolidge donated much of his correspondence to the Forbes Library in Northampton. The library has a special room to display Coolidge memorabilia.

## Silent Cal—Criticized and Admired Still

Coolidge once said, "The America which Washington founded does not mean we shall have everything done for us, but that we shall have every opportunity to do

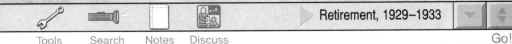
Tools    Search    Notes    Discuss                                    Go!

everything for ourselves."[4] He believed that it was more important to uphold existing laws than to create new ones. He did not sign many new laws into existence during his administration. Some people feel that government should play a more active role in the lives of the American people. They see Coolidge as a "do-nothing" president who accomplished little. Others think the federal government should not meddle in the lives of its citizens. They admire Coolidge for his hands-off policies.

▲ Coolidge was buried in the family plot at Plymouth Notch in 1933. His grave, pictured here, demonstrates his appreciation for simplicity and modesty.

Perhaps Coolidge will be best remembered for his personality. There are many stories about the shy and witty "Silent Cal." One tale tells of a woman who thought she could make Coolidge talk. "Oh, Mr. President," she said, "you are so silent. I made a bet today that I could get more than two words out of you." Coolidge replied, "You lose."[5]

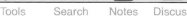
## Chapter Notes

### Chapter 1. Oath of Office, August 1923

1. Robert Sobel, *Coolidge: An American Enigma* (Washington, D.C.: Regnery Publishing, 1998), pp. 229–230.

2. Calvin Coolidge, *The Autobiography of Calvin Coolidge* (New York: Cosmopolitan, 1929), pp. 173–174.

3. Ibid., p. 175.

4. Claude M. Fuess, *Calvin Coolidge: The Man from Vermont* (Boston: Little Brown, 1940), p. 310.

### Chapter 2. The Early Years, 1872–1897

1. Robert Sobel, *Coolidge: An American Enigma* (Washington, D.C.: Regnery Publishing, 1998), pp. 22–23.

2. Calvin Coolidge, *The Autobiography of Calvin Coolidge* (New York: Cosmopolitan, 1929), p. 13.

### Chapter 3. Massachusetts Politics, 1898–1920

1. Robert H. Ferrell, *The Presidency of Calvin Coolidge* (Lawrence, Kans.: University Press of Kansas, 1998), p. 9.

2. Claude M. Fuess, *Calvin Coolidge: The Man from Vermont* (Boston: Little, Brown, 1940), p. 84.

3. George H., Mayer, "Coolidge, Calvin," *World Book Online Americas Edition,* <http://search.worldbookonline.com/wbol/wbPage/na/ar/co/132320> (August 14, 2001).

4. Ibid., p. 93.

5. William Allen White, *A Puritan in Babylon: The Story of Calvin Coolidge* (New York: Macmillan, 1938), p. 166.

### Chapter 4. Washington, 1920–1924

1. Robert H. Ferrell, *The Presidency of Calvin Coolidge* (Lawrence, Kans.: University Press of Kansas, 1998), p. 23.

2. John Hiram McKee, ed., *Coolidge Wit and Wisdom: 125 Short Stories about "Cal"* (New York: Frederick A. Stokes Co., 1933), p. 121.

3. Calvin Coolidge, *The Autobiography of Calvin Coolidge* (New York: Cosmopolitan, 1929), pp. 180–181.

4. Ferrell, p. 47.

Chapter 5. Elected President, 1925–1929

1. Robert Sobel, *Coolidge: An American Enigma* (Washington, D.C.: Regnery Publishing, 1998), p. 235.

2. Robert H. Ferrell, *The Presidency of Calvin Coolidge* (Lawrence, Kans.: University Press of Kansas, 1998), p. 61.

3. Ibid., p. 112.

4. William Allen White, *A Puritan in Babylon: The Story of Calvin Coolidge* (New York: Macmillan, 1938), p. 390.

5. J. R. Greene, *Calvin Coolidge: A Biography in Picture Postcards* (Athol, Mass.: Transcript Press, 1987), p. 68.

Chapter 6. Retirement, 1929–1933

1. Robert H. Ferrell, *The Presidency of Calvin Coolidge* (Lawrence, Kans.: University Press of Kansas, 1998), p. 204.

2. Calvin Coolidge, *The Autobiography of Calvin Coolidge* (New York: Cosmopolitan, 1929), p. 191.

3. Robert Sobel, *Coolidge: An American Enigma* (Washington, D.C.: Regnery Publishing, 1998), pp. 414–415.

4. John Hiram, McKee, ed., *Coolidge Wit and Wisdom: 125 Short Stories about "Cal"* (New York: Frederick A. Stokes Co., 1933), p. 139.

5. Ibid., p. 43.

Coolidge, Calvin. *The Autobiography of Calvin Coolidge.* New York: Cosmopolitan, 1929.

Curtis, Jane. *Return to These Hills: The Vermont Years of Calvin Coolidge.* Woodstock, Vt.: Curtis-Lieberman Books, 1985.

Feinstein, Stephen. *The 1920s From Prohibition to Charles Lindbergh.* Berkeley Heights, N.J.: Enslow Publishers, Inc., 2001.

Ferrell, Robert H. *The Presidency of Calvin Coolidge.* Lawrence, Kans.: University Press of Kansas, 1998.

Greene, J. R. *Calvin Coolidge: A Biography in Picture Postcards.* Athol, Mass.: Transcript Press, 1987.

Joseph, Paul. *Calvin Coolidge.* Edina, Minn.: ABDO Publishing Company, 1999.

Kent, Zachary. *Calvin Coolidge: Thirtieth President of the United States.* Chicago: Children's Press, 1988.

Stevens, Rita. *Calvin Coolidge, 30th President of the United States.* Ada, Okla.: Garrett Educational Corporation, 1990.

Wikander, Lawrence E. and Robert H. Ferrell, eds. *Grace Coolidge, An Autobiography.* Worland, Wyo.: High Plains Publishing, 1992.